HISTORY & GEOGRAPHY 407
MOUNTAIN COUNTRIES

Author:
Theresa K. Buskey, B.A., J.D.

Editor:
Alan Christopherson, M.S.

Assistant Editor:
Annette M. Walker, B.S.

Media Credits:
Page 3: © bgsmith, iStock, Thinkstock; **4:** © Skouatroulio, iStock, Thinkstock; **5:** © MisoKnitl, iStock, Thinkstock; **8:** © Dorling Kindersley, Thinkstock; **9:** © thewizzthatwoz, iStock, Thinkstock; **12:** © Claudio Gabriele Quercia, iStock, Thinkstock; © Łukasz Kurbiel, iStock, Thinkstock; **13:** © blackdovfx, iStock, Thinkstock; **14:** © Dorling Kindersley, Thinkstock; **16:** © irakite, iStock, Thinkstock; **17:** © Dorling Kindersley, Thinkstock; **18:** © OlgaCanals, iStock, Thinkstock; **19:** © Misha Shiyanov, Hemera, Thinkstock; **25:** © TimHesterPhotography, iStock, Thinkstock; **26:** © Daniel Prudek, iStock, Thinkstock; **27:** © Natallia Yaumenenka, iStock, Thinkstock; **29:** © Elena Belozorova, iStock, Thinkstock; **31:** © Avatar 023, iStock, Thinkstock; **32:** © master2, iStock, Thinkstock; **34:** © Muralinath, iStock, Thinkstock; © saashi, iStock, Thinkstock; **36:** © Dawid Markiewicz, iStock, Thinkstock; **38:** © Dorling Kindersley, Thinkstock; **40:** © Goodshoot, Thinkstock; **45:** © Robert Ford, iStock, Thinkstock; **47:** © elxeneize, iStock, Thinkstock; **48:** © Aleksey Trefilov, iStock, Thinkstock; **49:** © sculpies, iStrock, Thinkstock; **50:** © jacktheflipper, iStock, Thinkstock; **51:** © Elenarts, iStock, Thinkstock; **53:** © Stocktrek Images, Thinkstock; **55:** © MickeyNG, iStock, Thinkstock; **56:** © Pauws99, iStock, Thinkstock; **57:** © Maksim Halubchykau, iStock, Thinkstock; **58:** © AlexandrMoroz, iStock, Thinkstock; **59:** © Purestock, Thinkstock.

Alpha Omega
PUBLICATIONS

804 N. 2nd Ave. E.
Rock Rapids, IA 51246-1759

MOUNTAIN COUNTRIES

In this **LIFEPAC®** you will learn about life high in the tallest mountains. You will learn how people have adapted to the cold and thin air of the mountains. You will study Peru in the Andes of South America, Nepal in the Himalayas of Asia, and Switzerland in the Alps of Europe. You will learn about the country, the people there, and some of their history.

Objectives

Read these objectives. The objectives tell you what you will be able to do when you have successfully completed this LIFEPAC. Each section will list according to the numbers below what objectives will be met in that section. When you have finished this LIFEPAC, you should be able to:

1. Describe the basic geography of mountains.
2. Tell the location of the major mountain chains of the world.
3. Find Peru, Nepal, and Switzerland on a world map.
4. Tell the basic geography of Peru, Nepal, and Switzerland.
5. Tell the major cities, products, and languages of the three nations.
6. Tell the history of the three nations.
7. Describe the people and governments of the three nations.

1. PERU — THE ANDES

The Andes Mountains of South America seem to rise up out of the Pacific Ocean to block everything from reaching the continent. They are tall, dangerous mountains that once were the home of one of the greatest nations in the Americas. The Inca Empire grew to power among the Andes Mountains.

In this section, you will study the Incas and how they lived in the harsh mountains. You will also learn a little about the modern nation of Peru. But first you will learn some information about mountains all over the world.

Objectives

Review these objectives. When you have completed this section, you should be able to:

1. Describe the basic geography of mountains.
2. Tell the location of the major mountain chains of the world.
3. Find Peru, Nepal, and Switzerland on a world map.
4. Tell the basic geography of Peru, Nepal, and Switzerland.
5. Tell the major cities, products, and languages of the three nations.
6. Tell the history of the three nations.
7. Describe the people and governments of the three nations.

Vocabulary

Study these new words. Learning the meanings of these words is a good study habit and will improve your understanding of this LIFEPAC.

adapt (ə dapt'). To change to fit different conditions; adjust.

legend (lej' ənd). A legend handed down from the past, which many people believed, even if it was not true.

mortar (môr′ tər). A mixture of lime, cement, sand, and water for holding bricks or stones together.

terrace (ter′ is). A flat, raised piece of land with straight or sloping sides. They are often made one above the other in hilly areas to create more space for raising crops.

valley (val′ ē). Low land between hills or mountains.

viceroy (vīs′ roi). A person who rules a country, acting as the king's representative.

Note: *All vocabulary words in this LIFEPAC appear in* **boldface** *print the first time they are used. If you are unsure of the meaning when you are reading, study the definitions given.*

Pronunciation Key: hat, āge, cãre, fär; let, ēqual, tėrm; it, īce; hot, ōpen, ôrder; oil; out; cup, pu̇t, rüle; child; long; thin; /ℱH/ for then; /zh/ for measure; /u/ or /ə/ represents /a/ in about, /e/ in taken, /i/ in pencil, /o/ in lemon, and /u/ in circus.

Mountains

There are mountains on every continent and in every part of the world. Mountains are caused by two natural forces that God put in our world. Some mountains form where pieces of the surface of our earth push against each other. They push so hard that they push up, fold over, and break up to form mountains. Other mountains form when hot, liquid rock from deep inside the earth pushes up to the surface. These mountains are called volcanoes.

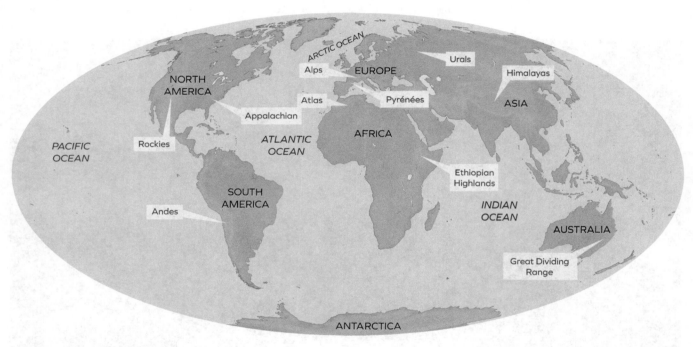

| World Mountain Ranges

 Map exercises.

1.1   Label the seven continents on the above map.

1.2   Circle the mountains that are closest to your home.

1.3   Put a square around the mountains that are on the border between Europe and Asia (they are in Europe and Asia).

Using the map, list the mountain ranges on each continent.

1.4   North America: _____

1.5   South America: _____

1.6   Europe: _____

1.7   Africa: _____

1.8   Asia: _____

1.9   Australia: _____

> ✓ **Teacher check:**
>
> Initials _____   Date _____

Altitude, or distance up into the air, is measured by how far it is down to the surface of the ocean, called *sea level*. When someone says that Mount Aconcagua is 6,960 meters tall, they mean that the top of the mountain is 6,960 meters above sea level. If someone says they were climbing at an altitude of 3,000 feet, they mean they were climbing on a mountain 3,000 feet above sea level.

Living in the mountains is more difficult than living down closer to sea level. There is less air to breathe in the mountains. That is because there is less and less air the higher you go in altitude. When you get high enough to reach outer space, there is no air at all! People can get altitude sickness going up into the mountains if they are not careful. They have trouble breathing, get a headache, and feel sick to their stomachs from the thin air.

However, God designed our bodies so that they can change and **adapt** to the thin mountain air. In fact, the bodies of people who live in the mountains are different in some ways from those people who live near sea level. Mountain people have bigger lungs to take in more air. They have more red blood cells that carry oxygen from the air to all the parts of their bodies. They also have bigger hearts so that more oxygen-rich blood can be pumped through their bodies.

Another problem with living in the mountains is the cold. Thin air does not hold heat as well as the thicker air near sea level, so the mountains are much colder than the land below them. Another problem is that mountains are also much windier. Mountains catch the winds that blow high up in the air around our earth. The wind makes it feel even colder than it really is. We call this *wind chill*. If you live in a place where it is cold, the weather forecaster will often report the wind chill in addition to the temperature in the winter.

One other problem in the mountains is that the thin air does not protect people from the sun. It is very easy to get a sunburn in the mountains. People who live in the mountains often have very tan skin from the sun.

As the air gets thinner going up a mountain, the climate changes. It is possible to have a hot, wet tropical rain forest at the bottom of a mountain and permanent snow and ice at the top! Usually, there is a forest of leafy trees near the bottom of the mountain. Higher up there is a second layer, a forest of pine trees which can live in colder, windier places. Above the pine trees is the tree line. The tree line is where the trees stop growing. It has become too cold and windy for them to live. Above the tree line is a third layer, tundra. This *alpine* tundra is very much like the arctic tundra in the polar regions. Above the tundra on high mountains is the snow line. From the snow line to the top of the mountain is the fourth layer, snow and ice that never melt all year.

Mountains affect the climate of the land around them, also. We have already studied how mountains block moisture from going over them. Winds blow wet air against one side of a mountain. The air gets cooler as it is pushed up the mountains. Cold air cannot hold as much water as warm air, so the water comes out of the air as rain. By the time the air gets all the way over the mountains, it is very dry. Very little rain falls on the other side of the mountains, which is called the rain shadow, and deserts often form there. Mountains very often have one side that is very wet and another that is dry.

The cool air in the mountains often causes the climate to be dry like in the Arctic and Antarctica. People, animals, and plants can still get water from streams made by the snow that melts in the short summers, so in spite of the cold, wind, and dry, thin air many kinds of life survive in the mountains.

The kinds of plants and animals that live on the mountains depend on how high up on the mountain you go. Nothing lives above the snow line. The plants and animals of the alpine tundra are very much like those

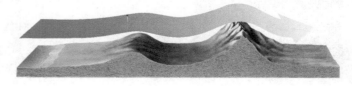

| Air pattern moving over mountains

in the arctic. The plants grow quickly in the summer, very close to the ground to stay warm. Several kinds of mouse-like animals gather summer seeds and grass, then hibernate through the long winter.

Most mountain ranges have some kind of wild goats or sheep that live there. Rocky Mountain goats live on mountainsides and are incredible climbers. They seem to be able to go up straight cliff walls! Bighorn sheep also live in the Rocky Mountains. The males fight each other by butting head to head with their thick horns. In Eurasian and African mountains, a type of goat called the Ibex, is found.

| Ibex

Lower down the mountains the plants and animals are like those in cool northern forests. Below the mountains the climate and wildlife will be correct for that place on earth. It could be desert, rain forest, or plains!
A trip up a mountain is like a visit to different climates stacked on top of each other.

Complete the following.

1.10   Altitude is measured by feet or miles above _____ .

1.11   List the four layers usually found on a mountain as you go up.

a. _____

b. _____

c. _____

d. _____

1.12 List four problems that make it difficult to live in the mountains.

a. _____

b. _____

c. _____

d. _____

1.13 The line between the forest and the alpine tundra is called the

_____ .

1.14 The line between the alpine tundra and the year-round snow is called them

_____ .

1.15 The animals and the climate _____ as you go up or down a mountain.

1.16 God designed people so that their bodies can _____ in thin mountain air.

Complete this activity.

1.17 On this mountain show the tree and snow lines by drawing in trees and snow where they belong. (The trees will become smaller and further apart as you climb higher on the mountain.)

Snow line →

Tree line →

Teacher check:

Initials _____   Date _____

The Andes and Peru

The Andes (an' dēz) Mountains are located in South America. They run all the way along the western coast of that continent. The mountain chain is about 4,500 miles (7,240 km) long. Driving the length of the Andes would be like driving from Cleveland, Ohio to Los Angeles, California and back! The highest mountain in the Andes is Mount Aconcagua in Argentina. It is 22,834 feet tall (6,960 m).

The country of Peru is in the Andes Mountains, just south of the equator. The capital is Lima (le' mə), a city on the Pacific (west) coast. This western side of the mountains is a narrow, dry plain that goes only along the coast of the Pacific Ocean. The Andes begin not far from the ocean. The plains along the coast are in the rain shadow of the Andes. Also, cold ocean water from Antarctica runs up along the coast, making the plains even drier. The area is a desert. Many rivers flow out of the mountains to the ocean. The people of Peru use the water to irrigate crops.

The mountains of central Peru are the source of the Amazon River. Melting snow in the southern part of the country forms

| Peru and its neighboring countries

rivers that run north through the mountain **valleys**. The Amazon flows out of Peru in the northeast into Brazil. That part of the country, on the wet eastern side of the mountains, is rainforest.

The central and southern part of the country is all mountains. The tallest is Mount Huascarán, at 22,205 feet (6,768 m) above sea level. High in those mountains on the border between Peru and Bolivia is Lake Titicaca. It is the largest lake in South America and the highest navigable lake in the world! It is 110 miles (177 km) long and about 35 miles (56 km) wide. It is 12,500 feet (3,810 m) above sea level.

The mountains provide Peru with a rich source of minerals. Copper, lead, silver, and zinc are all mined there. These minerals were one source of wealth for the mighty Indian nation that once ruled the Andes, the Inca.

Complete these sentences.

1.18   The western part of Peru is a _____ along the coast.

1.19   The south and central part of Peru is _____ .

1.20   The northeastern part of Peru is _____ .

1.21   The Andes run along the _____ coast of South America.

1.22   Peru is the source of the _____ River.

1.23   The highest navigable lake in the world is _____ in Peru.

1.24   The Andes of Peru are a rich source of _____ .

1.25   Mount _____ is the highest peak in the Andes.

The Incas

It was in Peru that the great Incan Empire began. "Inca" means chief or king and was the name of the ruler of the empire. We also use the name Inca to talk about the people.

The Incas believed in many, many gods. They believed their king was a descendant of the sun god and was also a god himself. Their **legends** say that the first Inca was sent by the sun, his father, to Lake Titicaca. The Inca was told to take a golden staff and walk until he found a place where the staff would sink into the ground. The Inca built his home at a spot where the staff disappeared completely in the ground. The place was named Cuzco.

| Lake Titicaca is the highest navigable lake in the world.

What we know happened is that the Incas settled in a rich mountain valley north of Lake Titicaca about 1,100 years after the birth of Jesus. There they started the city of Cuzco (küz' kō) which became their capital. Around A.D. 1438, the Incas began to fight and conquer the other people who lived around them. When they were finished, they had an empire that went from southern Columbia to central Chile, all of it in the Andes Mountains.

The Incas never invented writing. They kept all of their records on knotted strings called *quipu* (kē' pu). The sons of nobles learned in school to make records on quipu and how to read them.

All the land in the empire belonged to the king. The people only kept one-third of the food they grew. One-third went to the king, and another third went to the priests to serve the many gods. The king used his third to feed the army, the craftsmen, and anyone too ill or old to work. The people also had to work for the king so many days out of every year. The Incas used this "work tax" to build their cities and roads.

| Terrace farming

The Incas had to use all the land they could find to grow food for their huge empire. They used the work tax to build **terraces** to make level farmland on the sides of the mountains. They made the mountains look like giant stairways! They built canals to bring water to these farms.

In the valleys, bananas, oranges, and pineapples could be grown. The terraces on the lower parts of the mountains could be used to grow corn and beans. The terraces high up could grow potatoes and *quinoa* (ken' wä), a strong grain plant. The people of the Andes learned to make the potatoes into *chuño* (chü' nyo). Chuño is made by freezing the potatoes, mashing them, and then drying them in the sun. It will last for months without spoiling.

| Inca royalty

The Incas were skillful builders. They carved huge rocks by hand into blocks that fit together perfectly. They did not use **mortar** to keep the blocks together. Instead, they fit the stones together like the parts of a giant jigsaw puzzle. The stones were fitted so perfectly that not even a blade of grass can be pushed into the cracks. The Incas did such a good job that many of their walls are still standing today, even after many earthquakes!

The Incas also built roads all through their empire. The roads were paved with stone. They had to cross over deep, dangerous rivers in the mountains. The Incas built rope bridges over these rivers. The village nearest the bridge had to take care of it. About once a year, the villagers would weave new ropes and put up a new bridge.

The Incas used relay runners to send messages and small packages along their roads. All along the roads were small houses where runners waited. Messages were handed off from one runner to the next. The new runner would carry the message as fast as he could to the next house, where another runner would take it. The runners worked so quickly that the king could have fish run in from the Pacific Ocean for his dinner in Cuzco, halfway across the country!

Match these items.

1.26	_____ Inca	a.	lake where legends say the first Inca appeared
1.27	_____ quipu	b.	means king or chief
1.28	_____ Cuzco	c.	a collection of knotted strings used to keep records
1.29	_____ Titicaca	d.	used to grow food on mountainsides
1.30	_____ terraces	e.	capital of the empire

Answer these questions.

1.31 How was the food grown by the Incas divided?

_____

_____

_____

1.32 How did the Incas send messages across their empire?

_____

_____

_____

1.33 Where did the Incas get workers to build their roads and cities?

_____

_____

1.34 What was remarkable about the way the Incas built a wall?

_____

_____

The Incas did not have carts or horses. They used llamas (lä′ məs) as pack animals to carry heavy loads through their empire. The llama is related to the camel, but it lives at high altitudes in the Andes. Llamas have thick wool coats and can go without water for several days. They are very surefooted and can carry about 200 pounds (91 kg), but they do not carry people. The Incas made good use of the llamas, as do Peruvian people today.

| Alpacas

Female llamas produce milk, and llama meat is good to eat. Llamas produce wool that is spun into thread. Peruvian women today still spin the wool into thread, using a hand spindle as they walk or sit. The thread is woven into bright-colored cloth.

The alpaca (al pak′ ə) and the vicuña (vi kün′ yə) are related to the llama. They are smaller and not used as pack animals. The alpaca has finer wool that makes nicer cloth than llama wool does, but the best cloth of all comes from the wool of the vicuña. They are wild animals that must be trapped or killed to get their wool. Only the king and his family wore vicuña wool clothes in the time of the Incas.

The Inca nobles and the king lived in beautiful stone palaces with gardens. They often had running water brought in by copper pipes. The houses were decorated with many valuable things, some made of gold and silver. The Andes Mountains are rich in gold and silver. The Incas believed that gold was the sweat of the sun and silver the tears of the moon, and both were considered holy. Only the king and the nobles could wear gold. The Incas made beautiful jewelry, cups, plates, ornaments, and other objects of gold for their rulers.

The gold and silver attracted the Spanish, who came to the New World after Columbus. Some greedy men led by Francisco Pizzaro met the Incas in 1532. The Incas had heard about these bearded white men and were curious to meet them. Pizzaro kidnapped the Inca king and demanded gold and silver to free him. The king filled a room as high as he could reach once with gold and twice with silver, but he was killed anyway by the cruel Spaniards. Pizzaro then went on to conquer the Inca empire. The Incas had never seen horses or cannons and did not know how to fight them. A few of the people fought for years from cities higher in the mountains. The last Inca king was killed by the Spanish in 1572.

| Pizzaro and a room full of gold

Complete these sentences.

1.35   The Incas used _____ as pack animals.

1.36   Incas, and Peruvians today, weave cloth from the wool of

_____ , _____ , and _____ .

1.37   Only the royal family could wear clothes made from the wool of the

_____ .

1.38   The Inca made many beautiful ornaments and objects made of

_____ and _____ .

1.39   _____ kidnapped and killed the Inca king

before he conquered the empire.

Modern Peru

The Spanish ruled Peru for almost 300 years. The minerals there made it a very important colony. The riches went to Spain and to the Spanish people who moved to Peru. The Indians, descendants of the Incas, were forced to do all the work and were paid very little. They were often forced to work as slaves.

| Machu Picchu is an Incan village that Pizzaro missed in looting Peru of gold and silver and today is a very popular tourist destination.

Catholic priests reported back to the king in Spain about the cruel treatment of the Indians. The government officials in Spain were very angry when they heard about this. In 1542 the King of Spain signed a group of laws called the New Laws. These laws required the Spanish people in Peru to leave the Indians alone, but the new rulers of Peru did not want to obey the laws. They formed an army and killed the king's **viceroy** when he tried to enforce the laws. The next viceroy did not try to enforce the laws, but allowed the Spanish people to do what they wanted with the Indians.

Peru became independent of Spain in 1821, after José de San Martin of Argentina and Simón Bolívar of Venezuela led a revolt against all the Spanish rulers in South America.

Peru has been a *republic* (a country which elects its leaders) since it gained independence, but usually the president and leaders were very rich men who were of Spanish blood. Many times the military has taken control of the government and set up a dictator.

In 1990 the elected president, Alberto Fujimori, threw out the Congress and gave himself great powers. Later, he made a new constitution and again allowed a Congress to be re-elected, but Peru has never had good, dependable government like the United States.

President Fujimori was replaced in 2001 by Alejandro Toledo. Alan Garcia Pérez became president in 2006 and in 2011 Ollanta Humala became president.

Today, potatoes are still one of the most important food crops for the people of Peru. Other important food crops are corn and beans. They are often grown on the terrace farms that the Inca built. Fishing is an important industry. Fish are caught in the Pacific Ocean as well as Lake Titicaca. Peru is an important producer of fish meal.

| Woman wearing traditional clothes

Peru is trying to improve its government and businesses. It trades with many countries in the world. Its most important trading partners are the United States, Japan, Germany, and Brazil. Peru can send goods all the way down the Amazon River to the Atlantic Ocean as well as from its own ports on the Pacific. Peru has built many roads and railroads into the mountains to bring in goods and people. The Central Railroad climbs to 15,800 feet (4,815 m) as it goes through the mountains. That makes it the highest regular railroad in the world. However, the easiest way to travel to the cities of Peru is by airplane.

| Peruvian flag

The people of Peru speak Spanish and Quechua (kech' wə), the Inca language. About half of the people live in the *sierra*, as the mountains are called. Most of the people belong to the Roman Catholic Church, which was brought to Peru by the Spanish. Most of the wealthier people are of Spanish descent, while the Indians and people of mixed blood are usually poorer. Because of this, the poor people do not trust the government or the wealthy business owners. They feel they have no chance to succeed. It is difficult for a government to do a good job when the people do not trust each other. Peru's government must earn the trust of the people and give the poor the chances they need to succeed.

Answer *true* or *false*.

1.40 _____ The New Laws stopped the cruel treatment of the Indians.

1.41 _____ Peru has always had good, dependable government.

1.42 _____ The mountain part of Peru is called the *sierra*.

1.43 _____ Peru can send out goods on ships only on the Pacific Ocean.

1.44 _____ The people of Peru speak Portuguese.

1.45 _____ Most of the rich people in Peru are the Indians, descendants of the Incas.

1.46 _____ Peru became independent from Spain in 1821.

1.47 _____ José de San Martin and Simón Bolívar led the revolt that gave Peru independence.

1.48 _____ The Central Railroad in Peru is the highest regular railroad in the world.

1.49 _____ Farmers still grow potatoes on the Inca terrace farms.

Complete the puzzle.

1.50 Read the clues and write the words in the puzzle.

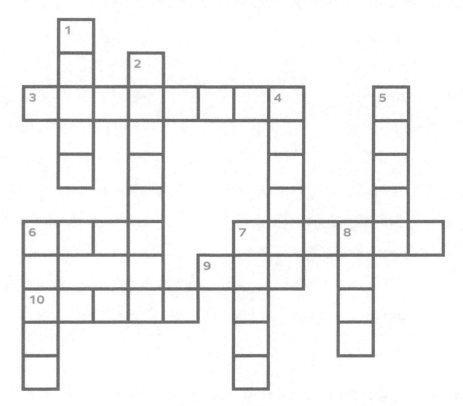

Across

3. The highest navigable lake in the world
6. The capital of Peru
7. _____ pipes brought water to Inca palaces.
9. In legend, the first Inca's father was the _____ god.
10. The mountains of Peru

Down

1. The way Incas kept records
2. Easiest way to travel to the cities of Peru
4. The great river that flows out of northeastern Peru
5. An animal the Incas had never seen before the Spanish came
6. The work animal of the Andes
7. The Incan capital city
8. The country we are studying

 Review the material in this section to prepare for the Self Test. The Self Test will check your understanding of this section. Any items you miss on this test will show you what areas you will need to restudy in order to prepare for the unit test.

SELF TEST 1

Match the correct answer with the word(s) (3 points each answer).

1.01	_____ sea level	a.	mountains of central Asia
1.02	_____ snow line	b.	river whose source is in Peru
1.03	_____ Amazon	c.	African mountains
1.04	_____ Urals	d.	European mountains
1.05	_____ Rocky	e.	altitude is measured from it
1.06	_____ Ethiopian Highlands	f.	above this is snow all year
1.07	_____ Great Dividing Range	g.	Australian mountains
1.08	_____ Himalayas	h.	North American mountains
1.09	_____ Pyrenees	i.	treeless slopes of the high mountains
1.010	_____ alpine tundra	j.	mountains that divide Europe and Asia

Choose the correct answer from the list below (3 points each answer).

sun god	llama	vicuña	Titicaca
gold	quipu	Cuzco	chuño
terraces	Francisco Pizzaro		

1.011 Legends say that the first ruler of the Incas was the son of the _____ .

1.012 _____ was the man who conquered the Incas for Spain.

1.013 The highest navigable lake in the world is Lake _____ , where legends say the first Inca appeared.

1.014 The Inca, and the people of Peru today, used the _____ to carry heavy loads.

1.015 _____ was the capital of the Inca Empire.

1.016   The Spanish were greedy to get the Inca _____ , "the sweat of the sun."

1.017   Incas used knotted ropes, called _____ , to keep records.

1.018   Only the Inca and the royal family could wear clothes made from the fine wool of the _____ .

1.019   The Inca built _____ , which are still used today, to farm the sides of the mountains.

1.020   Potatoes could be frozen, mashed, and dried into _____ , which would last for months without spoiling.

Answer these questions.

1.021   What are the problems people have living in the mountains? (2 points each answer)

a. _____

b. _____

c. _____

d. _____

1.022   What happens to the climate, animals, and plants as you go up a mountain? (3 points)
What is usually near the bottom? (1 point)
What is usually at the top? (1 point)

a. _____

b. _____

c. _____

1.023   On what continent and on what part of that continent would you find the Andes Mountains? (4 points)

_____

1.024   What did the Incas use the work tax for? (3 points)

_____

_____

_____

Answer *true* or *false* (2 points each answer).

1.025 _____ The Inca Empire covered all of South America.

1.026 _____ The Incas fitted walls together without mortar like jigsaw puzzles.

1.027 _____ The mountains of Peru are rich in minerals.

1.028 _____ Peru has had good, dependable governments since it became independent from Spain.

1.029 _____ Peruvians get wool, milk, and meat from llamas.

1.030 _____ Only the Inca king and the nobles could wear gold.

1.031 _____ The people of Peru speak Spanish and Quechua.

1.032 _____ Potatoes are no longer an important crop in Peru.

1.033 _____ Peru can ship goods to the Pacific or Atlantic Ocean.

1.034 _____ The New Laws passed by the King of Spain to protect the Indians were never enforced.

✔ **Teacher check:**

Score _____

Initials _____

Date _____

80 / 100

2. NEPAL — THE HIMALAYAS

Nepal is a small country in the Himalaya Mountains, the highest mountains in the world. Nepal had very little contact with the rest of the world until about 1950. It is a country where most of the people had never heard of a car, telephone, or airplane until only recently.

You will learn about the huge Himalayas in this section. You will also learn about the beautiful little country of Nepal. You will learn about their history, their government, and their people. You will also learn about Hinduism and Buddhism, the religions of Nepal.

Objectives

Review these objectives. When you have completed this section, you should be able to:

3. Find Peru, Nepal, and Switzerland on a world map.
4. Tell the basic geography of Peru, Nepal, and Switzerland.
5. Tell the major cities, products, and languages of the three nations.
6. Tell the history of the three nations.
7. Describe the people and governments of the three nations.

Vocabulary

Study these new words. Learning the meanings of these words is a good study habit and will improve your understanding of this LIFEPAC.

avalanche (av′ u lanch). A large mass of snow and ice, or dirt and rocks, rapidly sliding down the side of a mountain.

democracy (di mok′ rə sē). A government that is run by the people who live under it or through their elected representatives.

dynasty (dī′ nəs tē). A series of rulers who belong to the same family.

heartland (härt land). Center or most important land.

insecticide (in sek' tə sīd). A substance for killing insects.

landlocked (land lokt). Surrounded by land; having no seacoast.

monsoon (mon sün'). A wind that blows at certain times of the year in the Indian Ocean and Southeast Asia.

plaza (pläz' ə). A public square in a city or town.

porter (pôr' tər). A person employed to carry burdens or baggage.

protest (prō' test). A statement that denies or objects strongly.

temple (tem' pəl). A building used for the service or worship of a god or gods.

Pronunciation Key: hat, āge, cãre, fär; let, ēqual, tėrm; it, īce; hot, ōpen, ôrder; oil; out; cup, put, rüle; child; long; thin; /ŦH/ for then; /zh/ for measure; /u/ or /ə/ represents /a/ in about, /e/ in taken, /i/ in pencil, /o/ in lemon, and /u/ in circus.

Himalayas

The Himalayas are the highest mountain range on earth. The tallest <u>86</u> mountains in the world are there! The tallest mountain on earth is Mount Everest, which is 29,028 feet (8,848 m) tall. It is on the border between Tibet (part of China) and Nepal in the Himalayas.

| Mount Everest

The Himalayas run in a curve along the northern border of India. The word "Himalaya" means *House of Snow* in Sanskrit, an old Indian language. The range is about 1,500 miles (2,410 km) long, which is a little less than the distance between Los Angeles and Chicago. They separate China and India. Two countries, Nepal and Bhutan, lie in these mountains between India and China.

The Himalayas are so high that they kept the Indian and Chinese people separate from each other most of the time. It was like two neighbors who could not see each other because of a high wall. In fact, India is a peninsula that is cut off from the rest of Asia by the mountains. India is often called a *sub-continent* (something less than a continent) because it has water on three sides and high mountains on the fourth.

North of the Himalayas is the Tibetan Plateau. It is a large area of highlands in central Asia. The valleys in the plateau are often higher in altitude than mountains in other parts of the world. It is called "the roof of the world."

The Himalayas are in the tropical zone of the earth and receive **monsoon** rains every summer. The heavy rains come in from the Indian Ocean south of the mountains. The southern side of the mountains receives lots of rain. However, as with all mountains, the water in the clouds rain out as they move over the mountains. Therefore, the northern side of the mountains, especially the Tibetan Plateau, is very dry, with a desert-like climate.

The Himalayas are about as far north of the equator as Florida! At sea level the country is as warm as Florida. That means there is a very big difference between the bottom and the top of the mountains. The lower slopes in the south are covered with tropical rain forests. The climate and land change as you go up the mountains from leafy forest to pine forest to alpine tundra and, finally, to snow and ice. Many different kinds of plants and animals live in these different climates.

The Himalayas have many kinds of rhododendrons (rō də děn' drəns). "Rhodies" are small trees or bushes that have beautiful flowers in the spring. There are as many as 60 different kinds in the Himalayas. Some of those kinds grow as high up as the tree line!

The tahrs are a type of goat-antelope that lives in the Himalayas. They are a little over three feet tall and covered with beautiful thick fur. They live about halfway up the mountains. Blue sheep, on the other hand, live up in the alpine tundra. These wild sheep and goats are good climbers and are designed by God to live in their steep, cold homeland.

The most useful Himalayan animal for people is the yak. The yak is related to the North American bison (buffalo). They were created to live in the high mountains. They have thick, shaggy fur, and their bodies make good use of the thin air. The people of the mountains use yaks to carry loads just like the Andes llamas. Their outer fur is used for ropes, their inner fur for blankets, and their hides for all kinds of leather goods. Female yaks are called naks, and they produce a rich, creamy milk that is made into butter and cheese.

| A yak

Complete these sentences.

2.1   The countries of _____ and _____
       are in the Himalaya Mountains.

2.2   The Himalayas separate the nations of _____ and _____ .

2.3   The most useful animal of the Himalaya is the _____ .

2.4   North of the Himalayas is the _____ Plateau.

2.5   India is often called a _____ because it is surrounded
       by water and mountains.

2.6   Monsoon rains come to the Himalayas from (what direction?) _____ .

2.7   The highest mountain on earth is _____ .

2.8   The lower southern slopes of the Himalayas are covered with
       _____ .

2.9   The northern side of the mountains has a _____ climate.

Geography of Nepal

Nepal is a beautiful, **landlocked** country in the Himalaya Mountains between China and India. It is a rectangle-shaped nation which is a little bigger than Arkansas. The country's beauty and changes in climate attract many visitors.

The country is divided into three main areas that run across it in strips east to west like stripes. The stripe across the south is the *Tarai*. This is the rain forest plains in front of the mountains near India. Half of the people of Nepal live in this area, because it is the only good farmland in the country. Most of the country's food is grown there. However, people have been able to live there only recently. Before the invention of **insecticides**, it was too dangerous to live in the Tarai. The insects carried a deadly disease, malaria, that kept most people away.

The next stripe, across the center of the country, is the "hills" below the Himalayas. These hills would be considered mountains anywhere else on earth. This is the **heartland** of Nepal. This is where the country began, where the capital is, and what the people consider to be the most important part of their country.

| A monastery in Kathmandu

The hills are separated by deep valleys where the Nepali built their cities and grow much of their food. The Kathmandu Valley is where the nation began, and the capital, called Kathmandu, is there. The valley is surprisingly warm, in spite of the fact that it is 4,000 to 5,000 feet (1,200-1,500 m) above sea level. The temperature rarely goes below 40° F (4° C). For many years the name Nepal meant only this valley. Only since about 1960 has the name been used for the rest of the nation.

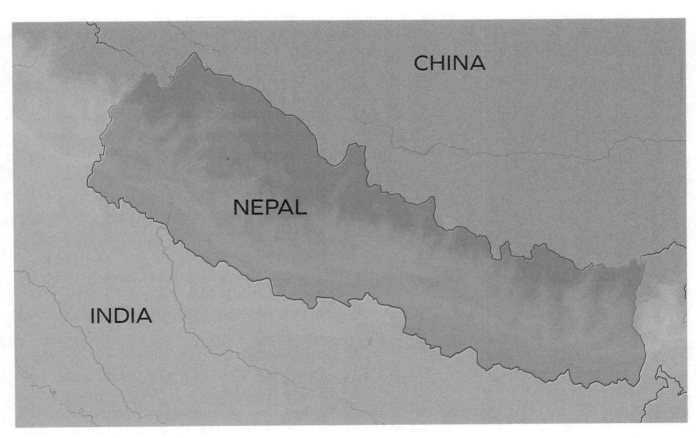

| Nepal and its neighbors

The most northern stripe is the high mountains of the Himalayas. Eight of the ten tallest mountains in the world, including Mount Everest, are there.

Only a very small part of the people live there. They live mostly in small villages that can only be reached by hiking trails. They live by farming small pieces of terraced land, herding animals (yaks, sheep, and goats), and by trading with the people in the valleys. This is the part of the country that attracts mountain climbers and hikers from all over the world. Many of the mountain people earn a living guiding and carrying supplies for the climbers.

| Nepalese flag

Use the text and map to answer these questions.

2.10 What country is north of Nepal? _____

2.11 The Tarai is next to what country? _____

2.12 Why did people not live in the Tarai until recently?

_____

_____

_____

2.13 What are the three regions of Nepal?

a. _____

b. _____

c. _____

2.14 How many of the ten tallest mountains in the world are in Nepal? _____ .

2.15 List four things the mountain people do to make a living.

a. _____

b. _____

c. _____

d. _____

The Country of Nepal

History. The history of Nepal is the history of the Kathmandu Valley. So few people lived in the Tarai and the mountains that the valley was the country. Even today, mountain people traveling to the capital will say they are going to Nepal.

Around the time Jesus was alive, the valley was an important trading center. Wool blankets, yak products, and carpets from Tibet were traded with India. This trade continues today.

Many different families of kings, called **dynasties**, ruled the Kathmandu Valley. The first known dynasty was the Kirati (or Kirats), who ruled the valley from about 700 years before the birth of Jesus until 300 years after his birth. We know very little about that family and what they did

|Nepalese holy man

in the valley. The second family known to rule the valley was the Licchavi, who ruled for about 550 years after the Kirati dynasty. These kings brought in the religion of *Hinduism*, which will be described later.

After the Licchavi, no one ruled the valley for about 400 years. The valley was divided into small kingdoms and towns that fought with each other. Many different dynasties ruled the kingdoms, but by about A.D. 1200 the valley was divided into just three kingdoms, ruled by kings called *Mallas*. During this time, the Nepali created many beautiful buildings and paintings. The kings built palaces, **temples**, statues, and **plazas** to beautify their cities. These works of art are still enjoyed by visitors to Nepal today.

The Malla period lasted until 1768, when the three Malla kingdoms were conquered by a new dynasty, the Shah family. The Shah kings conquered the land around them and created a nation that was twice as big as Nepal is today. In 1814, though, they fought a war with the British, who were ruling India. The British stopped the Nepali army and made the country the size it is now.

After being defeated by the British, Nepal closed itself off from outsiders. Very few Europeans were allowed to visit. The same was true of Tibet to the north. As a result, Nepal and the Himalayas were the last places on earth except Antarctica to be mapped.

| Nepal temple and plaza

Between 1846 and 1951, the Shahs remained as kings, but they lost their power. Another family, the Rana family, became the actual rulers. They let the king keep his title, but he was kept under guard and did not control the government. The Rana were very corrupt. They ran the country only to make money for themselves and did not want the Europeans to stop them. They worked hard to keep Europeans and their ideas of good government out of the country.

However, the Rana could not stop the world from reaching them. After World War II, India became independent from Britain. Nepal had always traded with India, and the new Indian government wanted Nepal to change; so the government of India helped the Shah king to escape in 1950. The people of Nepal then forced the Rana out of power, and the king returned. It is the Shah family that rules in Nepal as of 2004.

Nepal tried to set up a type of government, which has a Congress and a king, called a constitutional monarchy. Britain has that type of government. But Nepal's king did not like sharing power with an elected government, and in 1960, he arrested the elected head of the government (the Prime Minister) and forced the Congress to stop meeting.

The king ruled Nepal by himself until 1990. Many people did not like the fact that they could not elect people to run the government. They led protests against the king. In 1990, many protesters died when soldiers shot them as they gathered around the Royal Palace. The king finally agreed to allow elections, and the Nepali elected new leaders in 1991. Nepal was a Constitutional monarchy from 1990-2008.

During the Constitutional monarchy the government was challenged by many groups, both inside and outside of the government. It was also challenged by problems within the Shah family itself.

The position of Prime Minister was unstable during this time with 14 different leaders in 18 years.

In 2001 the crown prince of Nepal shot most of his family, including his father, the king, and then shot himself. The king's brother was named the new king. In 2002 King Gyanendra dismissed the Congress, who had been elected by the people, and assumed power himself. He was deposed as king in 2008 when the Constitutional monarchy was abolished and the country became a Federal Republic. The head of state is the President and the government is managed by the Prime Minister who is appointed by the Parliament.

Match the following family names with the description.

2.16 _____ Shah

2.17 _____ Malla

2.18 _____ Rana

2.19 _____ Licchavi

a. ruled three kingdoms in the valley and built beautiful buildings

b. still kings of Nepal as of 1997

c. brought Hinduism to Nepal

d. kept the kings under guard and did not allow them to run the government

Answer *true* or *false*.

2.20 _____ Many different families have ruled the Kathmandu Valley.

2.21 _____ The Rana welcomed Europeans into Nepal to help the people.

2.22 _____ Nepal became a constitutional monarchy again in the 1990s.

2.23 _____ Nepal never has traded with India.

2.24 _____ The Shah king escaped to India to get away from the Rana.

Religion. The main religion of Nepal is called Hinduism. It was brought in from India by the Licchavi dynasty (which came from India). Hinduism is a very difficult religion to understand. It is especially difficult for Christians, who are used to the simple message of Jesus that all who believe in Him will be saved.

There are three main Hindu beliefs you need to know. First of all, the Hindus believe that when they die they are born again as someone or something else on earth. If they have been good, they will be reborn as a wealthier or more important person. If they have been bad, they will be reborn as a poorer person or an animal. They can also be reborn as a god if they are very good.

Secondly, Hindus believe in many, many, gods. These gods have also died and been reborn, and each god can be worshiped as any one of the many lives he lived. So Hindus worship gods all the time, in many places and ways. They made **idols** (what the Bible calls graven images), statues of the gods they worship. They will give the statue food, flowers, bathe it, or put clothes on it. They do this to get the god to protect them or do something for them. For example, the elephant-headed god, Ganesh, is supposed to bring good luck if he is pleased with what is offered to his statue. Also, making offerings is one of the good things a Hindu can do to get a better rebirth.

Along with the gods, Hindus also believe in demons and evil spirits. They must make offerings to the gods and to the spirits to stop bad things from happening. Illness, an accident, or a problem at work will be blamed on an evil spirit or failure to make the gods happy. A good Hindu must be sure to please all the gods and spirits.

| Ganesh

| Young girl praying

HISTORY & GEOGRAPHY 407

LIFEPAC TEST

NAME _____

DATE _____

SCORE _____

80 / 100

HISTORY & GEOGRAPHY 407: LIFEPAC TEST

Write *S* in the blank if the statement is about Switzerland, *P* if the statement is about Peru, and *N* if the statement is about Nepal (2 points each answer).

1. _____ The Red Cross was started here.

2. _____ People raise llamas.

3. _____ People raise yaks.

4. _____ The Inca people built roads and cities.

5. _____ People raise cows and goats.

6. _____ Hinduism is the most important religion.

7. _____ This country is in Asia.

8. _____ Cheese-making is an important, modern industry.

9. _____ Protestants and Catholics are about equal in number.

10. _____ This country is in Europe.

11. _____ This country is rich in minerals.

12. _____ Bern is the capital.

13. _____ Kathmandu is the capital.

14. _____ It was against the law to teach about Jesus in the 1990s.

15. _____ Spanish is one of the important languages.

Match these places with their descriptions by writing the letter of the place in front of the correct description (2 points each answer).

16. _____ mountains of south Switzerland   a. Himalayas

17. _____ river that starts in Peru   b. Alps

18. _____ mountains of Peru   c. Amazon

19. _____ great city of the Incas   d. Andes

20. _____ city where John Calvin worked   e. Cuzco

21. _____ mountains of north Switzerland   f. Geneva

22. _____ mountains in Africa   g. Tibetan Plateau

23. _____ mountains of Nepal   h. Jura

24. _____ roof of the world, Asia   i. Blanc

25. _____ tallest mountain in the Alps   j. Atlas

Complete each sentence using a word from the list (3 points each answer).

Titicaca	Constance	William Tell	Francisco Pizzaro
Gurkha	Sherpa	John Calvin	St. Bernard
Lima	Edmund Hillary		

26. Lake _____ is in Peru.

27. Lake _____ is in Switzerland.

28. The _____ are Nepali people famous as mountain guides and porters.

29. The _____ are Nepali people famous as soldiers.

30. _____ was a Swiss hero.

31. _____ was a leader of the Reformation.

32. _____ is the capital of Peru.

33. _____ conquered the Inca Empire.

34. _____ was one of the first two men to climb Mount Everest.

35. Monks have helped travelers in the _____ Passes for over a thousand years.

Answer *true* or *false* (2 points each answer).

36. _____ The coast of Peru is along the Pacific Ocean.

37. _____ Switzerland is landlocked.

38. _____ Lake Geneva is in Nepal.

39. _____ The people of Nepal worship idols.

40. _____ Nepal is a wealthy country.

41. _____ The Incas kept records on carved stone plates.

42. _____ The Ural Mountains are in Africa.

43. _____ Only the Inca nobles and kings could wear the fine wool of the vicuña.

44. _____ Nepal has a king.

45. _____ Secrecy laws helped to make Swiss banking successful.

46. _____ The Romans called Switzerland *Suisse*.

47. _____ Tourism is an important source of money for Nepal.

Thirdly, Hindus believe that everyone is born into a *caste*, or group, that they cannot get out of during *this* life. A person born into a caste must do the work of that caste. If you are born into the caste that sweeps the streets, that is what you must do all your life.

Important caste people cannot eat with or even touch lower caste people. If you are in a low or unimportant caste, it is believed you deserved it because you were evil in your last life. Thus, it is hard for Hindus to improve their lives if they are poor. Wealthy, important people usually will not work with or help poor, unimportant people. Poor people have no hope of working hard and making their lives better. They can only make offerings to the gods and hope to be reborn into a better caste in their next life.

Eventually, if a Hindu is good enough through many lives, he will reach the top of the ladder in rebirths. The best that can happen to a Hindu is to stop being reborn and become a part of the greatest god or spirit. When that happens, the person no longer exists. He just disappears and becomes a part of the universe. That is the closest Hinduism comes to salvation.

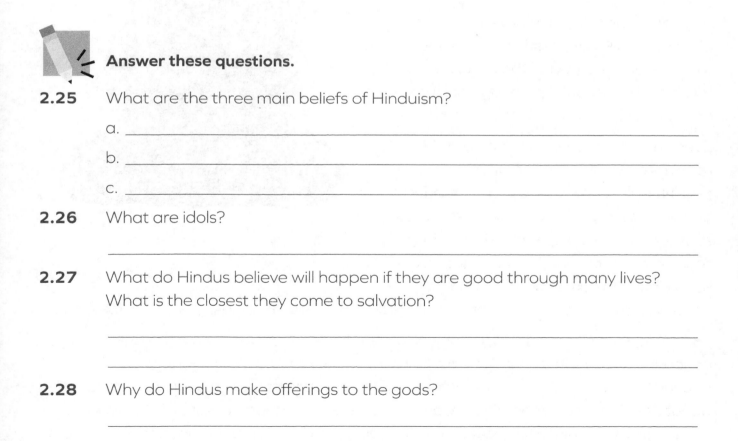

Answer these questions.

2.25 What are the three main beliefs of Hinduism?

a. _____

b. _____

c. _____

2.26 What are idols?

_____

2.27 What do Hindus believe will happen if they are good through many lives? What is the closest they come to salvation?

_____

_____

2.28 Why do Hindus make offerings to the gods?

_____

_____

Buddhism is the other main religion of Nepal. Buddhism also came from India. It was created about 1,500 years ago by a high-caste Indian man who did not like Hinduism. He decided what people needed to do was stop desiring the food, pleasures, and things of this world. If they made themselves stop wanting things, people would become free of the cycle of death and rebirth. That was what this man, called Buddha, believed.

Both Buddhists and Hindus believe in being reborn as someone else on earth. Buddhists do not have castes, and they believe you can escape rebirth by self-control in this life. Buddhists also worship many gods and spirits, including Buddha.

In Nepal, the Buddhist and Hindu beliefs are mixed together. Buddhists do not worry about caste, but they do join in the worship of Hindu gods. The Hindus join in the Buddhist ceremonies, too. They try to please <u>all</u> the gods. But most of the country is Hindu, and the leaders are always Hindu.

| Buddha

Religion is very important to the people of Nepal. They have festivals all year for the different gods. All of their art is about religion. The beautiful paintings, statues, and rugs are to honor different gods.

Every important event in a person's life requires a ceremony or an offering to a god. Nepali people also check with priests or religious leaders to find the best day to start planting crops, get married, or begin something important. They cannot rest, like a Christian can, knowing that Jesus has saved them. They must work hard to earn the gods' blessings.

For a long time Christianity was not welcome in Nepal. The Nepali saw the British conquer India, and they did not trust Christians. They thought Christianity was a way to conquer their land. The law in Nepal said that Christians were not allowed to teach about Jesus and salvation. There were some Nepali Christians in spite of the old laws. After Nepal was named a secular state in 2008 the door has been open to evangelism.

Complete these sentences.

2.29   The man who created the religion of Buddhism is called _____ .

2.30   Buddhists, like Hindus, believe in _____ as someone else on earth.

2.31   In Nepal, Buddhists and Hindus worship each other's _____ .

2.32   For many years it was against the law to teach about _____

in Nepal.

2.33   Buddhists believe people can escape being reborn if they stop

_____ .

People. The people of Nepal come from many different tribes or groups, perhaps as many as a hundred. Each of these groups has its own separate language, culture, and history, but the people are united by the Hindu and Buddhist religions. Most of the people speak Nepali, the national language, in addition to the language of their own group.

Two of the groups are famous outside of Nepal. One of the famous groups are the Gurkhas. The word "Gurkha" is the name of the city the Shah family ruled before it conquered Nepal. The name is used for the hardy men who served in the Shah's army. The British who fought their army in 1814 were very impressed with how well the soldiers fought. They were so impressed that they began hiring the soldiers of Gurkha to serve in the British army. At that time the British had colonies all over the world and needed good soldiers for its army.

The Gurkhas were and are strong, capable men who grew up in the "hills" of Nepal. They are known all over the world as very good fighters. Gurkha regiments in the British Army have fought in every major war in this century. They received many medals for bravery in World Wars I and II. Even today, many Nepali men earn a good living and a nice retirement pension by serving in the British army.

The second famous group is the Sherpa people. The Sherpas live in the Himalayas around Mount Everest and the other high peaks. They are famous for their strength, good humor, and knowledge of the mountains. They guide and help the expeditions that climb the mountains. Their skills were discovered by the European expeditions that came to try to climb Mount Everest in the early 1900s.

There are no roads leading to Mount Everest. Everything a group needs to live and climb has to be carried in by **porters**. The Sherpas are able to carry large loads of supplies up steep mountains on their backs. They also help the climbers survive in the dangerous mountains. When a huge storm hit the Everest area in 1995, the Sherpas were able to save the lives of many of the trapped climbers.

Europeans tried for years to climb Mount Everest. **Avalanches**, thin air, winds, and steep slopes caused many failures. A British expedition finally succeeded in 1953. Sir Edmund Hillary, a New Zealander, and Tenzing Norgay, a Nepali Sherpa, were the first two men to stand on top of the world's tallest mountain.

Most of the people of Nepal still live by farming. They grow rice, maize, oilseed, jute (which is a plant used to make rope, burlap sacks, or mats), and sugar cane in the tropical Tarai. Rice, millet, barley, and maize are grown in the hills. In the mountains, buckwheat, barley, and potatoes (brought from America in the 1700s) are grown. Most of the farmers keep a few animals as well. Highlanders often have large herds of yaks that must be moved from summer to winter pastures.

| Sir Edmund Hillary and Tenzing Norgay climbing Mount Everest

The mountains are terraced, as they are in the Andes, to create as much farmland as possible. In the dry areas of the Himalayas, water must be brought in by irrigation canals from streams of melting snow. Even so, the highlanders usually need to trade with the valley people or work for a time as a porter to have enough food for the whole year.

Complete these sentences.

2.34 The _____ are people who are famous as mountain guides and porters.

2.35 The foods grown in the tropical Tarai are _____ , _____ , _____ , _____ , and _____ .

2.36 The _____ are famous as soldiers in the British army.

2.37 Most of the people of Nepal live by _____ .

2.38 Foods grown in the high mountains are _____ , _____ , and _____ .

2.39 The first men to climb Mt. Everest were _____ and _____ .

Nepal Today

Nepal is one of the poorest countries in the world. It has very little industry, no important minerals, and few roads. There is one major road running into India and one to China from the Kathmandu Valley. There are also some roads connecting major cities. Most of the roads are in the flat Tarai region. Most of the country has <u>no</u> roads. The smaller towns and villages, especially in the hills and mountains, can only be reached by walking trails. Everything must be carried in on the backs of porters or yaks.

Nepal is too isolated and difficult for most industries to reach. The people are too poor to buy what the industries make, and it is too expensive to ship it somewhere else. Some cloth production has been set up. Hand-woven wool rugs have become a popular export and provide some income.

Tourism is one of the biggest sources of income for Nepal. The beautiful countryside and high mountains attract visitors from all over the world. Airplanes that can land and take off on short runways (usually fields) can carry some of the tourists into the mountain areas.

But, most of the tourists walk or "trek" to see the country. The Nepali people have set up lodges (little restaurant/hotels) for these hikers along the most popular trails. Some of the people, especially the Sherpa, serve as guides or porters or people traveling on the trails.

Money comes to Nepal from other countries in the form of aid. This is money that other countries give or loan to help Nepal. The money might be used to build roads, hospitals, airports, or schools. The employment of Gurkha soldiers is an important source of money, too. The soldiers send home part of their salaries for their families and spend their retirement pensions once they come home.

Very few Nepali receive an education. Less than two out of every five adults can read and write. Girls in particular are rarely ever sent to school. Even if a person gets a college education, there are very few jobs for them because there are so few businesses.

| Sherpas carrying supplies

Many people in Nepal do not get enough to eat. That is especially true in the highlands because food does not grow well there and it is expensive to porter more up from the valleys. Because of diseases and the lack of food, most people die before they are 55 years old. A woman who has six children usually has at least one die as a baby.

The Nepali people do not understand how to handle trash. They never had plastics and cans that don't rot when they are thrown away. A guide will often throw empty food cans into the nearest river after he serves a tourist's dinner. Litter has become a problem on the popular trails. Water is polluted because trash and other waste is dumped into the rivers.

A bigger problem is the cutting down of the Nepali forests. The people use the wood for firewood. Especially in the cold mountains, fires are needed for heat as well as cooking. Cutting down the trees without replacing them leaves the soil unprotected. The good soil needed for crops washes away in the heavy monsoon rains. Also, once the trees are gone, there will be no more firewood.

Nepal's government is trying to help with these problems, but they have very little money to use to solve them. The government also has many dishonest people who do not do their jobs. So Nepal is a very beautiful land with very big problems.

Answer *true* or *false*.

2.40 _____ Most of the towns and villages in Nepal are connected by roads.

2.41 _____ Tourism is an important source of income for Nepal.

2.42 _____ Litter and water pollution are problems in Nepal.

2.43 _____ Foreign countries do not help Nepal.

2.44 _____ People in Nepal often go hungry.

2.45 _____ Nepal has many industries and businesses.

2.46 _____ Cutting down trees in Nepal is good.

Review the material in this section to prepare for the Self Test. The Self Test will check your understanding of this section and will review the first section. Any items you miss on this test will show you what areas you will need to restudy in order to prepare for the unit test.

SELF TEST 2

Match the correct answer with the word (2 points each answer).

2.01	_____	Urals
2.02	_____	Sherpas
2.03	_____	Gurkhas
2.04	_____	Appalachian
2.05	_____	Atlas
2.06	_____	Titicaca
2.07	_____	Andes
2.08	_____	Tibetan
2.09	_____	India
2.010	_____	Everest

a. mountains between Europe and Asia

b. mountains of North America

c. plateau in central Asia, the roof of the world

d. African mountains

e. South American mountains

f. called a subcontinent

g. tallest mountain on earth

h. Nepali people famous as mountain guides

i. highest navigable lake in the world

j. Nepali people famous as soldiers

Write an _N_ on the line if the statement is true of Nepal or a _P_ if it is true of Peru (2 points each answer).

2.011	_____	in the Himalaya Mountains
2.012	_____	in the Andes Mountains
2.013	_____	as of 1997, the Shah dynasty still reigns there
2.014	_____	Hinduism is the most important religion
2.015	_____	Buddhism is an important religion
2.016	_____	Roman Catholicism is the most important religion
2.017	_____	it is landlocked
2.018	_____	the Inca Empire began there
2.019	_____	goods can be shipped out on the Atlantic or Pacific Ocean
2.020	_____	the mountains are rich in minerals

Answer these questions (5 points each answer).

2.021   Why did the Spanish want to conquer the Incas?

_____

_____

_____

2.022   What is the most important mountain animal for the people of Nepal? Why?

_____

_____

_____

2.023   What is the most important mountain animal for the people of Peru? Why?

_____

_____

_____

2.024   What are the three regions of Nepal?

a. _____

b. _____

c. _____

Answer *true* or *false* (1 point each answer).

2.025   _____   Nepal is a very wealthy country today.

2.026   _____   The Nepali people usually receive a good education.

2.027   _____   Buddhists and Hindus believe they will be reborn as someone or something else on earth after they die.

2.028   _____   The Andes are the tallest mountains on earth.

2.029   _____   Nepal became a democracy again in about 1990.

2.030   _____   For many years it was against the law to teach about Jesus in Nepal.

2.031   _____   Nepali people do not think their religion is important.

2.032 _____ The high mountain people can easily grow plenty of food in the mountain soil.

2.033 _____ Tourism is an important source of money in Nepal.

2.034 _____ People in Nepal often go hungry.

Choose the correct answer from the list below (3 points each question).

Kathmandu	Cuzco	Lima	monsoon
Rana	caste	idols	Edmund Hillary
quipu	Francisco Pizzaro		

2.035 _____ conquered the Inca Empire for Spain.

2.036 The _____ family kept the kings of Nepal under guard and would not let them have any power.

2.037 The Incas used knotted strings called _____ to keep records.

2.038 Hindus are born into a group or _____ and cannot get out of it in this life.

2.039 _____ is the capital of Peru.

2.040 _____ is the capital of Nepal.

2.041 _____ was the capital of the Inca Empire.

2.042 Hindus worship statues called _____ .

2.043 _____ was one of the first two men to climb the tallest mountain in the world.

2.044 Nepal gets rain from the Indian Ocean when the _____ comes.

Teacher check: Initials _____

Score _____ Date _____

80 / 100

3. SWITZERLAND — THE ALPS

Switzerland is a small, freedom-loving country in the center of Europe. It is protected by two different mountain chains, the Alps and the Jura. On the high plain between those mountains, the Swiss people have built a rich, successful nation.

In this section you will learn about the Swiss nation, its proud history, and its success. In spite of its poor resources, Switzerland is one of the richest nations in the world. You will learn why the Swiss are so well off and what their land is like.

Objectives

Review these objectives. When you have completed this section, you should be able to:

3. Find Peru, Nepal, and Switzerland on a world map.
4. Tell the basic geography of Peru, Nepal, and Switzerland.
5. Tell the major cities, products, and languages of the three nations.
6. Tell the history of the three nations.
7. Describe the people and governments of the three nations.

Vocabulary

Study these new words. Learning the meanings of these words is a good study habit and will improve your understanding of this LIFEPAC.

confederation (kən fed' ə rā' shən). A joining together of states, groups, or countries for a special purpose.

constitution (kon' stə tü' shən). The basic rules according to which a country, state, or group is governed.

international (in' tər nash' ən əl). Having to do with two or more countries.

jagged (jag' id). With sharp points sticking out.

militia (mə lish' ə). An army of citizens who are not regular soldiers but who are trained for war or any other emergency.

monk (mungk). A man who gives up everything else for religion and lives in a place with other men who do the same.

natural resource (nach' ər əl rē' sôrs). Materials supplied by nature.

neutral (nü' trəl). On neither side in a quarrel or war.

Protestant (prot' is tənt). A member of any of certain Christian churches which split off from the Roman Catholic Church.

rebellion (ri bel' yun). An act of resistance; a revolt.

reform (ri fôrm'). To make better; improve by removing faults.

refugee (ref' yü jē). A person who must leave a country for safety.

representative (rep' ri zen' tə tiv). A person appointed or elected to act or speak for others.

transportation (trans' pər tā' shən). Means of carrying things from one place to another.

Pronunciation Key: hat, āge, cãre, fär; let, ēqual, tėrm; it, īce; hot, ōpen, ôrder; oil; out; cup, pu̇t, rüle; child; long; thin; /FH/ for then; /zh/ for measure; /u/ or /ə/ represents /a/ in about, /e/ in taken, /i/ in pencil, /o/ in lemon, and /u/ in circus.

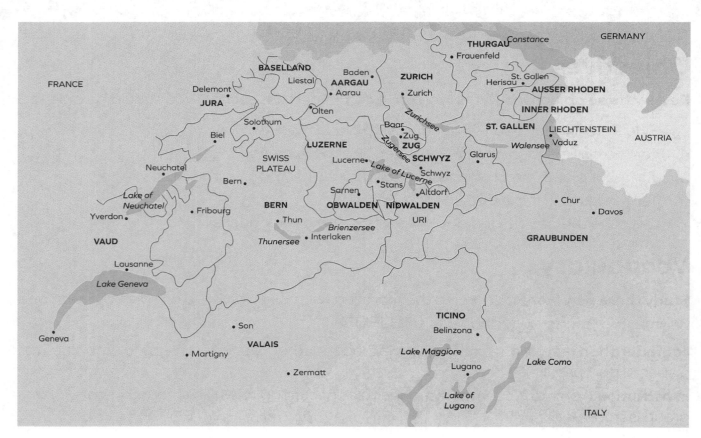

| Switzerland

The Alps and Switzerland

The Alps are the largest chain of mountains in Europe. They are not as tall as either the Andes or the Himalayas. They run along the northern part of the country of Italy. The mountains also cover a small part of southeastern France, most of Switzerland, a small part of southern Germany, and a large part of western Austria. The entire chain is about 750 miles (1,200 m) long. That is about the distance between New York City and Chicago, Illinois.

The tallest mountain in the Alps is Mount Blanc. It is 15,771 feet (4,807 m) tall. The Matterhorn is another Alpine mountain that is not so tall. It is famous because it is difficult to climb. Climbers reached the top of Mount Blanc 80 years before anyone climbed the Matterhorn!

| The Matterhorn

The Alps are famous for their **jagged** peaks and steep valleys. People come there from all over Europe and the world to ski, hike, and explore. Mountain climbing became popular in the Alps in the 1800s. Most of the tall peaks in the Alps were climbed for the first time in the middle of that century.

Switzerland is a landlocked nation in the Alps, about the size of Connecticut and Maryland combined. Its capital is the city of Bern. The Alps cover a large part of southern Switzerland. A chain of smaller mountains called the Jura run along the northern border. In between the two mountain ranges is the Swiss Plateau. Most of the people live in the plateau area.

Switzerland is famous for its many beautiful mountain lakes. The biggest ones are Lake Constance on the border with Germany and Lake Geneva on the border with France. These two lakes are at either end of the Swiss Plateau. There are hundreds of lakes in between them.

Switzerland has many streams and rivers fed by the melting snow and glaciers. Many of the important rivers of Europe have their source in the Swiss Alps. The Rhine, the Rhône, and the Inn River (which joins the Danube) begin there.

People cross the Alps by using passes, low places between the mountain peaks. The most famous are the two Saint Bernard Passes between Italy and Switzerland. **Monks** have lived up there for over a thousand years, keeping a house for travelers to rest and be safe in the dangerous mountains. These monks raised St. Bernard dogs to locate and rescue travelers who were lost in the snow. Today, most people cross the Alps using highways, railroads, and tunnels through the mountains. Today's travelers are in little danger from the mountains. The monks still live up in the passes, though, and tourists often visit them in the summer.

| St. Bernard dog

The mountains of Switzerland have very few minerals that can be mined to make money. The one important **natural resource** the Swiss do have is their swift-moving rivers. They use the rivers to make electricity to run their industries and businesses.

The steep sides of the mountains make avalanches a danger in Switzerland. Sometimes a warm wind called the *foehn* (fen) blows from the south. It hits the sides of the mountains and quickly melts the heavy snow. This causes large piles of snow to slide down the mountain, crushing everything in their path.

| The *Bernina Express* travels on the highest railway transversal in the Alps.

Complete these sentences.

3.1 _____ is the capital of Switzerland.

3.2 When the *foehn* blows there is a great danger of an _____ .

3.3 The mountains of north Switzerland are the _____ .

3.4 The area between the two mountain chains in Switzerland is called the

_____ .

3.5 The tallest mountain in the Alps is Mount _____ .

3.6 Lake _____ and Lake _____

are at either end of the Swiss Plateau.

3.7 Switzerland's one important natural resource is the swift-moving _____ .

3.8 The monks in the _____ Passes have helped travelers

for over a thousand years.

Swiss History

The Swiss are a freedom-loving people with a long, proud history of fighting for their independence. Switzerland was part of the great Roman Empire that ruled Israel at the time Jesus was born. In fact, Rome ruled all the land around the Mediterranean Sea and most of the west part of Europe. They called Switzerland *Helvetia*, after a tribe of people who lived there. That name is still used on Swiss money today.

| Flag of Switzerland

After the Roman Empire fell apart, Switzerland was ruled by the Franks. The Franks were an important tribe that founded the countries of France and Germany. Eventually, the Swiss came to be controlled by the Austrians.

The Swiss did not like Austrian Emperors ruling their land. In 1291 three *cantons*, which are like states, or the original thirteen colonies in America, agreed to fight together to protect themselves from the emperor. These three cantons around Lake Lucerne were the beginning of the Swiss **Confederation**. One of these cantons is named *Schwyz*, from which we get the name Switzerland.

One legend from this time is about a Swiss hero named William Tell. William Tell refused to bow to a pole set up by the emperor's official in the canton of Uri. The official forced Tell to shoot an apple off of his son's head with a crossbow as a punishment. Tell hit the apple safely, but told the official he had a second arrow to kill him if the boy had been hurt. The official imprisoned William Tell, who later escaped and led the war against the emperor.

| Demonstration of William Tell's tale

We do not know if the story of William Tell is true, but we do know that the brave Swiss fought many battles to win and keep their freedom. They became famous as fighters all over Europe. The new country grew bigger as more cantons joined and more land was taken in battles. In 1515 the Swiss were defeated by the French when they were fighting in Italy. The Swiss decided they did not want to win more land and fight wars in other countries. They decided to be **neutral** in all wars. The Swiss people have kept that policy for almost 500 years now.

About the same time the Swiss decided to become neutral, great changes were taking place in Europe. The Roman Catholic Church was the only Christian church in Europe for over a thousand years. The church had become rich and powerful. The leaders no longer followed the Bible. The people of Europe became angry and began the *Reformation*. The Reformation was a **rebellion** against the Catholic Church and a **reform** of Christianity all over Europe. Preachers began to teach the Bible instead of church laws and rules. Many new churches that we know today like the Lutheran and Baptist Churches were created.

Two great leaders of the Reformation lived and worked in Switzerland. John Calvin preached and worked in the city of Geneva. Huldreich Zwingli led the Reformation in the city of Zurich.

The **Protestants** of Switzerland, the people who left the Catholic church, fought many battles with those people and cities that stayed in the Roman church. Neither side could defeat the other, so both lived together in Switzerland. All of Europe fought a huge war, called the Thirty Years War, when the Catholics tried to force the Protestants to give up their faith. Neither side won in that war either, so Europe also kept both Protestants and Catholics. Switzerland stayed neutral and was finally recognized as an independent nation by all of Europe when the war ended in 1648.

| John Calvin with other reformers on the Reformation Wall in Geneva

Complete these sentences.

3.9 The _____ was the great change that ended the power of the Roman Catholic Church over all of Europe.

3.10 The Roman Empire called Switzerland _____ .

3.11 In the story of _____ , he is forced to shoot an apple off of his son's head.

3.12 _____ were the people who left the Catholic Church.

3.13 _____ was a great Reformation leader in Geneva, while _____ worked in Zurich.

3.14 The _____ War was the great war fought in Europe between the Catholics and the Protestants.

3.15 After losing a battle in 1515, the Swiss decided to be _____ in wars.

3.16 The Swiss are a _____ -loving people.

3.17 Swiss states are called _____ .

3.18 The Swiss Confederation was formed to fight against the Emperor of _____ .

The cantons in Switzerland were very independent until the late 1700s. People thought of themselves as citizens of their canton, not of their country. The national or federal government did not have much power. Most decisions and laws were made by the cantons.

France conquered most of Europe, including Switzerland, around the end of the 1700s. The French ruler, Napoleon, made the federal government very strong and called the country the Helvetic Republic. Napoleon was eventually defeated, and the nations he conquered were given their freedom. Switzerland returned to its old style of government by the cantons, but not for very long.

The people of Switzerland wanted to be more united and to reform their government. In 1848 they accepted a **constitution** that set up a strong federal government. They changed it again in 1874. That is the constitution they still use today. (The American Constitution was accepted in 1788.)

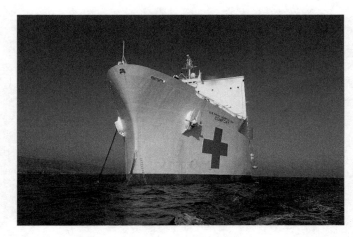

| Hospital ship with the Red Cross insignia

Switzerland stayed neutral while World War I (1914-1918) and World War II (1939-1945) raged across Europe. Many **refugees** fled to Switzerland during the wars. Switzerland also made money trading with and doing work for both sides in the wars.

Many **international** groups have had their offices in Switzerland over the years because the country is neutral. The League of Nations, set up to protect world peace, was set up in Geneva, Switzerland after World War I. The International Red Cross, which helps people in need all over the world, was started in Switzerland and still has its main offices there. In fact, the symbol of the Red Cross is the Swiss flag with the colors reversed. The Swiss flag is a white cross on a red background, while the Red Cross flag is a red cross on a white background.

The Swiss people have kept an armed neutrality, which means they are always ready to fight if they must. All young men are part of the **militia**. They spend time learning how to fight as soon as they are old enough. They keep their uniforms and weapons in their homes while they work their regular jobs. If anyone attacked Switzerland, the men would all be ready to fight quickly. One of the reasons Switzerland was not attacked during World War II, was because they had explosives ready to blow up the passes leading into the country to stop any invaders.

Because of their neutrality, Switzerland did not join the United Nations, the world peace organization created after World War II. However, many of the United Nations offices in Europe are in Switzerland. The Swiss also have refused to join the European Union which is trying to unite the countries of Europe into one large country. The Swiss have stayed independent. They like it that way.

Answer *true* or *false*.

3.19 _____ The Swiss fought on the side of England during World War II.

3.20 _____ Switzerland does not ever prepare to fight because it is neutral.

3.21 _____ Switzerland did not join the United Nations or the European Union.

3.22 _____ The Swiss cantons were very independent before the late 1700s.

3.23 _____ The International Red Cross has its main offices in Switzerland.

3.24 _____ Switzerland has never been conquered by another nation.

3.25 _____ The Swiss use a constitution that was accepted in 1704.

Complete this activity.

3.26 The Red Cross flag is a red cross on a white banner. The Swiss flag is a white cross on a red banner. Correctly color the Swiss flag and the Red Cross flag.

Swiss Flag

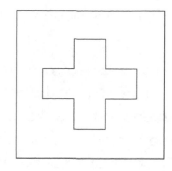

Red Cross Flag

Teacher check:

Initials _____ Date _____

Switzerland Today

Government. As of the late 1990s, the Swiss Confederation (the country's official name) had twenty-three cantons.(Three of these were so big that they were divided into half-cantons). Each canton has a local government and sends **representatives** to the federal government. All people 18 or older can vote for their representatives, just like in the United States.

| Bern, the capital of Switzerland

Unlike the United States, however, the people of Switzerland do not vote for a president. The parliament, the Swiss Congress, chooses seven people to run the government as a group. One of those men is chosen as the president for just one year, then another takes his place.

Like the states in America, the cantons make many of their own laws about different things closer to home than the things the federal government makes laws about. The cantons, for example, control education of children. The federal government controls only college education. All children are required to go to school from ages seven to sixteen. Almost all Swiss people can read and write.

Many of the cantons have been passing laws by voting for hundreds of years. A few of them still vote the way they did long ago. The people of the town gather together in the main square, then someone reads the law. The people vote for or against it by raising their hands!

Languages. The people of Switzerland speak four different languages! They speak German, French, Italian, and Romansh. Romansh is very much like Latin, the language of the old Roman Empire. Only a small number of people in one canton still speak it.

Because of the languages, Switzerland has three official names. *Schweiz* is the German name. *Suisse* is the French name, and *Svizzera*, is the Italian name.

The German language spoken in Switzerland is not like the German spoken in Germany. In fact, it is so different that Germans have a very hard time understanding someone who speaks *Schwyzerdütsch*, Swiss German, but both countries use the same written German. More than half of the people of Switzerland speak German. Most of the books, newspapers, movies, and television shows are in German.

People. The people of Switzerland are hard-working. The Swiss and the Americans live according to ideas taught during the Reformation. The leaders of the Reformation taught that hard work is good. All work is blessed by God if it is done for His glory. Because the ideas of the Reformation were important in both Switzerland and the United States, both countries believe that hard work is good and should be rewarded.

| Pole with the coats of arms of the 26 cantons of Switzerland with the Swiss flag in the center

The people of Switzerland today are about evenly divided between Protestants and Catholics. The government protects their right to worship any way they choose. A small number of people follow non-Christian religions or no religion at all.

Swiss people have written many famous books, mostly in German. The books of John Calvin, the Reformation leader who lived in Geneva, are considered to be some of the most important in the history of Christianity. One author you may have heard of is Johanna Spyri. She wrote *Heidi*, a wonderful story about a Swiss girl whose love helped many people.

Match these items.

3.27	_____ Suisse	a.	Swiss German
3.28	_____ Schwyzerdütsch	b.	German name of Switzerland
3.29	_____ Romansh	c.	Latin-like language
3.30	_____ Svizzera	d.	Italian name of Switzerland
3.31	_____ Schweiz	e.	French name of Switzerland

Answer *true* or *false*.

3.32 _____ Switzerland has 32 cantons.

3.33 _____ Johanna Spyri wrote *Heidi*.

3.34 _____ The people of Switzerland are very hard-working.

3.35 _____ The Swiss president is elected by the people every four years.

3.36 _____ Most of the Swiss people are either Protestant or Catholic.

3.37 _____ Swiss German is the same as the German of Germany.

3.38 _____ Very few Swiss people go to school.

Business. The country of Switzerland, like Nepal, has very few resources; however, the Swiss people are among the wealthiest in the world, while the Nepali are among the poorest. One reason for the difference is that Switzerland is surrounded by modern, wealthy European nations that can trade with it. The other reason is the people themselves. The Christian Swiss serve a God who loves them and wants them to succeed. He honors their work. The Hindu Nepali serve gods who are selfish and want offerings before they will help them. Moreover, the Hindu Nepali are supposed to deserve whatever life they have. They cannot work to change it without getting into trouble with their religion. Thus, two countries with the same kinds of problems have very different results.

| Milk cheese on shelves

The Swiss land is no better for crops than any other mountain land we have studied. In fact, Switzerland buys most of its food from other countries. The Swiss do, however, have land for grazing animals. They raise many, many brown cows and goats for their milk. Most of the milk is made into cheese. The Swiss are famous for their many kinds of delicious cheese. Most of it is made in large, modern factories and sent all over the world. The Swiss also make some of the world's best chocolate.

Switzerland has many important industries. They must buy the parts from other countries to make their goods, which makes their goods expensive. They must be very well made, or people will not pay the high prices for them. One type of industry the Swiss are very famous for making is watches and clocks. Swiss watches are very expensive, but they are also well-made and keep perfect time.

| Swiss watches are among the best in the world.

Watchmaking began in the Jura Mountains of northern Switzerland. Small factories are found in the little towns all over the region. It used to be that farmers would tend their animals in the morning and evening and make watches during the day. Even today, Swiss watches are often made by hand by skilled craftsmen.

The Swiss are also well known for other types of equipment that must be very exact. They make and sell to other countries many kinds of items that are needed for accurate or careful work. They make things such as electronic equipment, special tools, and **transportation** equipment. Most of their factories are small, and there are many of them all over the country. In fact, they do not have enough people to do all the work they have to do. People come in from other countries to get good jobs in Switzerland.

Another major business in Switzerland is banking. The city of Zurich is the banking center of the country. For years the Swiss had very, very strict laws that allowed people to deposit money secretly in their banks. Because the country is neutral and therefore safe from changes in government, people trusted the banks. They also knew that no one could find out where their money was or how much they had because of the secrecy laws. However, many criminals took advantage of the laws to hide money they made illegally. Today, some of the laws are changing so that money from criminals can be found and removed.

| Skiing in Switzerland

Like Nepal, Switzerland also makes money from tourism. The number of visitors every year is more than the population of the country! Most people come to ski in the winter. They also come to see the beautiful Alps, which are the best-known part of this busy, successful country.

Complete this activity.

3.39 Check the items that are important goods or services from Switzerland.

_____ chocolate   _____ cheese

_____ rugs   _____ wheat

_____ silver   _____ watches

_____ banking   _____ fishing

_____ tourism   _____ electronic equipment

Answer _true_ or _false_.

3.40   a. _____ Switzerland and Nepal are both poor countries.

b. _____ The Swiss grow many crops but do not raise many animals.

c. _____ Swiss watchmaking began in the Jura Mountains.

d. _____ Swiss goods must be well made before people will buy them
because they are so expensive.

e. _____ Swiss banking laws used to keep bank information very secret.

Before you take this last Self Test, you may want to do one or more of these self checks.

1. _____ Read the objectives. See if you can do them.

2. _____ Restudy the material related to any objectives that you cannot do.

3. _____ Use the **SQ3R** study procedure to review the material:

a. **S**can the sections.

b. **Q**uestion yourself.

c. **R**ead to answer your questions.

d. **R**ecite the answers to yourself.

e. **R**eview areas you did not understand.

4. _____ Review all vocabulary, activities, and Self Tests, writing a correct answer
for every wrong answer.

SELF TEST 3

Match the correct statement with the name (2 points each answer).

3.01 _____ Zurich

3.02 _____ Blanc

3.03 _____ Andes

3.04 _____ Himalayas

3.05 _____ Jura

3.06 _____ Helvetia

3.07 _____ Joanna Spyri

3.08 _____ John Calvin

3.09 _____ William Tell

3.010 _____ Alps

a. mountains of Nepal

b. mountains of north Switzerland

c. reformation leader in Geneva

d. mountains of Peru

e. banking city

f. wrote *Heidi*

g. Swiss hero

h. mountains of south Switzerland

i. highest mountain in the Alps

j. Roman Empire's name for Switzerland

Choose the correct answer from the list below (3 points each answer).

avalanche	rivers	St. Bernard	Swiss Plateau
Constance	Reformation	Zwingli	neutral
cantons	Bern		

3.011 _____ is the capital of Switzerland.

3.012 The _____ was a rebellion against the Catholic Church and a reform of Christianity in Europe.

3.013 Monks have kept a house for travelers in the _____ Passes for over a thousand years.

3.014 Swiss states are called _____ .

3.015 The one major natural resource the Swiss have is their _____ , which they use for electricity.

3.016   Switzerland is a _____ country which does not take sides in wars.

3.017   The _____ is in between the two mountain chains of Switzerland and is where most of the people live.

3.018   Lake _____ is on the border between Switzerland and Germany.

3.019   The *foehn* can cause an _____ when it blows in from the south.

3.020   _____ was a leader of the Protestants in Zurich.

Answer this question (3 points each answer).

3.021   What are three of the languages of Switzerland?

  a. _____

  b. _____

  c. _____

Name the country we have studied that best matches the statement (3 points each answer).

3.022   Country most like the United States _____

3.023   The major religions are the most different from the United States

   _____

3.024   Country located closest to the United States _____

3.025   Country in the highest mountains _____

3.026   Country with the most mineral resources _____

3.027   Country with the best history of freedom _____

Check the items that are important goods or services of Switzerland (1 point each answer).

3.028   a. _____ gold   b. _____ cheese

c. _____ tourism   d. _____ steel

e. _____ chocolate   f. _____ watches

g. _____ banking   h. _____ fishing

i. _____ coal   j. _____ corn

Answer *true* or *false* (1 point each answer).

3.029   _____   The Swiss Confederation began when the people rebelled against the Austrian Emperor in 1291.

3.030   _____   Switzerland did not fight in World War II.

3.031   _____   Switzerland has a king.

3.032   _____   The Thirty Years War was fought by Switzerland against Italy in 1920.

3.033   _____   The Swiss have a militia to defend themselves against invaders.

3.034   _____   Mount Everest is the tallest mountain in the world.

3.035   _____   The Rocky Mountains are in North America.

3.036   _____   The Tibetan Plateau is called the roof of the world.

3.037   _____   It is against the law to teach about Jesus in Switzerland.

3.038   _____   There are very few industries in Switzerland.

3.039   _____   The Inca was a ruler in Nepal.

3.040   _____   The Sherpa are people famous as mountain guides.

3.041   _____   India is on the southern border of Peru.

Teacher check: Initials _____   **80**

Score _____   Date _____   **100**

Before you take the LIFEPAC Test, you may want to do one or more of these self checks.

1. _____ Read the objectives. See if you can do them.
2. _____ Restudy the material related to any objectives that you cannot do.
3. _____ Use the **SQ3R** study procedure to review the material.
4. _____ Review activities, Self Tests, and LIFEPAC vocabulary words.
5. _____ Restudy areas of weakness indicated by the last Self Test.

NOTES

NOTES

NOTES

NOTES